THE LEADERSHIP WARRIOR: COACHES EDITION

LESSONS FROM THE SAMURAI

A four-week practice in authentic leading and living

By Alison Arnold, PhD

ISBN-978-0-692-98370-6
Published by Head Games Sports, LLC
1678 North Edgewood Street, Flagstaff, AZ 86004

To my family,
You inspire me to keep stretching.

To the coaches that strive to be better,
Thank you for changing the world, one
athlete at a time.

Also by Dr. Alison Arnold

FEAR–Tame the Beast
A workbook and video program for athletes

Doc Ali's Tight Mind Tool Deck
51 simple tools for gymnasts to build an unshakeable mind

The Athlete Warrior
Advanced Mental Training for the Advanced Athlete

**The Most Important Job in the World:
Parenting Your Athlete DVD**

Train Your Mind Visualization
Audio CD & Download

Scream and Run Naked
Lessons from a Neurotic's Journey to Nepal

For more information about Dr. Alison Arnold
or for additional resources, visit:

www.HeadGamesWorld.com
www.HeadGamesWebCamp.com
or call her directly at *602-284-8077*

This book is a simple practice. It's a simple practice in waking up to the leader you are, one day at a time for four weeks. They say it takes 28 days to change a habit. This is the habit changer. If you are like me, you fall asleep easily.

What I mean is, even though you try to make changes in your life, your personality, your actions that don't serve you, the old ways come back and haunt you again and again. This small practice is your snooze alarm, designed to wake you again and again. It's the call to wake up and be the type of leader you were meant to be. There is no time to waste as the world and everyone in it needs your leadership.

They need it now.

Many of us in coaching have gotten too comfortable. We say what we want, we lose our temper. Sometimes we inadvertently make fun of athletes making them feel small and bad about themselves. Being a coach and being a leader is taking full responsibility for your role in the lives of the athletes you coach. Imagine yourself as an energy imprint. With everything you say and do your athletes feel your impact on them. When you are proud they feel it, when you are angry or disappointed they feel it, too. Starting now, take full responsibility for your actions in the gym. Look carefully at how you effect the kids you coach. Most importantly, look carefully at yourself. Are your words or actions building up the character of your athletes, or breaking them down, filling them with self-doubt, questions, and labels that will last a lifetime.

This is the way of the Samurai. The Samurai (or Bushi) were noble members of the military class beginning during the 12th century. They were the Japanese warriors. Samurai were supposed to lead their lives according to the ethic code of Bushido ("the way of the warrior").

Strongly Confucian in nature, Bushido stressed concepts such as loyalty, self-discipline and respectful, ethical behavior. Our four-week practice will implement some of the concepts from the way of the warrior, many of which are still very applicable today.

I suggest you read each daily quote, exercise, and the mantra for the day in the morning when you are fresh. After reading and doing any writing the practice suggests, sit quietly and repeat the mantra ten times in your head while breathing deeply. Use this mantra throughout the day to help you wake up to the practice of the Samurai leader.

The word Samurai comes from the Japanese verb "saburau," meaning to serve or attend. Samurai translates as servant. For the next four weeks, you are practicing the art of being the servant leader. Servant leaders devote themselves to serving the needs of organization members, developing people and bringing out the best in them, coaching others and encouraging their self-expression, facilitating personal growth in all they lead, giving honest feedback in constructive ways, and listening to others and building community.

This type of Samurai leadership has a combination of warrior characteristics (loyalty, respect, ethical behavior, and discipline) and servant characteristics (selflessness, nurturing, empowering). The integration of these forces leads to the ultimate excellence in leadership. We desire nothing less.

Enjoy the process. Work the practice.

道程 訓練

姿勢

Day One
ATTITUDE

"The greatest discovery of all time is that a person can change his future by merely changing his attitude."
—*Oprah Winfrey*

You are the one who creates the climate of those around you. At the beginning of this process it is essential that you take responsibility for your life.

How can you see life as one big adventure? All events that happen in your day today are neutral. It is the attitude you take to those events that create them as "good" or "bad."

The ultimate leader remains positive in the face of adversity. The ultimate leader has an attitude of optimism even through daily challenges. I call this "relentless optimism." Relentless optimism is finding the gift in every challenge. It's never giving up on an athlete no matter how frustrated you feel. If they keep making mistakes, you remain with your eyes on the prize. If they keep balking with fear, you remind them of previous challenges they have overcome. Your language is one of the ultimate cheerleader, "I know you can do this. You just haven't made it YET." "Let's keep working, back it down, and get some successful drills." Relentless optimism is intense. But every sentence is motivated by the essence of belief that your athlete can be even better than they are right now.

How can you view every situation that happens to you today as one that has been put on your path to help you grow and be a better coach?

We are beings of energy. As a leader, your energy can be felt through the entire gym, even throughout your entire organization. Like a stone that is thrown into a pond, your attitude ripples through every person you come in contact with.

Commit today to make your energy one of positivity, relentless optimism, and action. Be sure your interaction with the athletes and coaches around you reflects the characteristics you want them to feel about themselves. If you want them to feel confident, treat them as if they are gifted. If you want them to be kind, treat them with kindness. If you want them to be motivated, motivate them!

Today, model the attitude you want to have as a leader for the next 30 days of this program.

Below, choose six words that describe the coach you want to be.

1.

2.

3.

4.

5.

6.

Place these words somewhere you can see them during the entire day. Then, inhabit those words with all your being. All it takes is discipline. All it takes is a change in your own attitude.

Mantra:
All events are neutral. I choose my attitude.

Day Two
AWARENESS

"I think self-awareness is probably the most important
thing towards being a champion."
—*Billie Jean King*

In order to change anything about yourself, you have to be
aware of yourself. The first step in being the ultimate coach
is becoming more aware of who you are and how you impact
those around you.

When one is unaware there is a tendency to react to life,
to rely on defenses and habits to lead the way. Awareness
gives you the power to make choices about how you want
to respond. Is this the way I want to react to this situation?
Does this represent the coach I want to be?

Most of our habitual reactions come from our ego. The ego is
the part of us that wants to prove we are good, accomplished,
and powerful. We want to be recognized for our accomplishments and feel special. Coaching from ego tends to produce
desperation, leading you to coach from a place of fear. Let's
say you had a great season with your team last year. Your
ego says, "I'd better do it again or people will say what a bad
coach I am." Or if your athletes make mistakes during a
competition the ego says, "People will think I'm not good
enough to coach this level." Coaching from ego leads to
reactions like yelling, threats, shaming, belittling, and sarcasm,
which ends up hurting the athlete and the environment in
the gym.

Today, look at your habitual reactions to situations. How do you feel when the athletes are moving too slow during practice? Or when the same athlete has the same fear again and again?

Watch yourself from the observer point of view. Almost as if you were watching yourself as a character in a movie. Imagine that everything you do or say is being broadcast on that big screen in Times Square. Do you feel proud of what's coming out of your mouth? Would the parents of your athletes approve? When you can begin to detach from your habits and emotional reactions, then you have power over them. This is the power of awareness.

Developing the ability to observe yourself without being caught up in the drama is one of the most important tools of the ultimate leader. When you are caught up in emotional drama, there is no awareness. Only habitual reactions probably programmed as early as the childhood years.

Keep practicing this "movie-view" of your life. See yourself as the hero or heroine and watch the affect you have on others. In stressful situations, use your breathing to slow down, get present, and get out of ego.

Are you aware of how you come across to other people? Today, ask someone you trust how you come across as a leader and coach. It can be a little scary to really ask for honest feedback, but push yourself to be open and nondefensive. Be sure to tell this person that you really want the feedback, and their responses will be taken constructively and treated with highest regard. Do not punish a person who has the courage to give you honest feedback!

Think of three questions that can help you understand yourself better and ask three people. Here are some examples:

1. What are my greatest strengths as a coach?

2. What can I do better as a coach?

3. What is one thing you notice about me that I might not be aware of?

Awareness is key to any coach who want to see excellence in themselves and others.

Mantra:
I am aware of who I am and how I affect others in everything I do.

均衡

Day Three
BALANCE

"Life is like riding a bicycle. To keep your balance
you must keep moving."
—*Albert Einstein*

A table with three legs has a very unstable foundation. It cannot stand, bear weight, or weather a storm. This is also true of a leader without balance. When you are out of balance, so is the rest of your team. Being ragged and weary is not the sign of good leadership. It is the sign of a poor life manager.

I've heard many excuses from poor coaches about why they are out of balance: "I'm too busy." "No one can do what I do." "Things would fall apart if I didn't take care of these things." These excuses are simply ways people who don't feel important try to feel important. Do something different. Really make yourself important and do something for yourself.

When you are out of balance and not taking care of yourself, you become angry. It's that simple. A coach that doesn't take care of himself always harbors some sort of resentment. This resentment shows up in the gym during stressful situations. Your athletes seem to be cutting corners during conditioning, and instead of figuring out a way to raise their level of excellence you yell, "I'm tired of your lack of effort!" An athlete is late to practice, and instead of asking them what happened you say, "Go with the lower level group, you missed too much already."

Today, do something small to take care of yourself and let the people around you know you are doing it. Even taking a walk outside to clear your head and get some fresh air can be helpful. Go out to a nice lunch, put on your favorite music in the office, get your nails done, or tell the front office that you are taking ten minutes to relax before the second half of your workout.

Ultimately, it is these small things that will give you the patience and strength you need to be a great leader. Without taking care of yourself, you can't be there for your athletes or staff in the way you want. It's impossible to hold a good attitude through the trials and tribulations of your day if you are depleted and exhausted. Give to yourself, so you can give to others. Make it a priority you commit to without compromise.

Mantra:
I deserve to take care of myself.

Day Four
BOUNDARIES

"Don't tell people how to do things; tell them what
to do and let them surprise you with their results."
—*George S. Patton*

There are two types of boundaries great leaders should be
aware of: expectations and limits.

A great leader has clear expectations of the people that
surround him. It's essential that people around you know what
you want, expect, and even demand from them. People rise
to the level of the leader's expectation. Sometimes people in
leadership positions allow their people to run all over them.
At other times they run their program like a dictatorship.
Neither of these are true leaders.

When the athletes around you know what you expect from
them, they actually perform better. The structure gives them
a guideline to strive for, to meet and possibly surpass your
expectation.

We've all seen the consequences of over-permissive parenting.
Kids that have a sense of entitlement, believing they can get
away with anything. That is what happens when a leader or
parent has no boundaries.

Today, be sure your colleagues, staff, and athletes know what
you as a leader expect from them. Are your requirements
clear? Are they known by the people around you? If not, it

may be time for a meeting or conversation. Sit down with your people and go over what you expect from them. Behavior, performance, etiquette, and commitment level are all fair game. Be sure to spell it out in black and white. And remember, they will meet or exceed your expectations, so don't set the bar too low.

Not only does a coach need to set boundaries in terms of expectations, they also needs to set boundaries as a coaching professional. Coaches are teachers and should maintain the professional boundary of a teacher/student relationship. You are not their friend, confidant, or parent. You are a teacher. With everything you do, this professional boundary must be adhered to. Be aware of setting firm boundaries with yourself on what are appropriate coaching behaviors. Do you text your athletes? Do you engage in group social media channels? How much do they know about your personal life? How do you treat fellow coaches? Do you talk about parents, coaches, or other athletes in front of your athletes? Do you tease them in ways that could be perceived as hurtful? Do you go to certain athletes' birthday parties but not others? Are there other ways you play favorites?

These questions could go on and on but the bottom line is, are your actions congruent with the highest professional standards of teachers? Ask yourself, "If I were to say this comment or do this action in the public school system, would I still have a job?" Practice having impeccable boundaries.

On the next page, write any loose boundaries you could tighten up as a leader. Examples include: I lose my temper in front of the athletes. I coach some kids more than others. I criticize kids to my co-coach in front of other athletes.

Mantra:
I have impeccable boundaries in terms of expectations and limits. I know at the core I am a teacher.

Day Five
COMMITMENT

"Individual commitment to a group effort – that is what makes a team work, a company work, a society work, a civilization work."
—Vince Lombardi

What is your commitment level as a coach? Are you as committed as the athletes around you? A leader cannot expect their athletes or staff to have a higher level of excellence, put in more hours, be more organized, or show more discipline than she models.

What are the important things you would like to see from your athletes in terms of commitment? In the space below write five things that would demonstrate a higher level of commitment from your staff or athletes. Then ask yourself, "Am I doing these things?"

Today, spend one day being sure you are modeling each of your five commitments. Challenge yourself to continue this practice for more than just the day.

Commitments:

1.

2.

3.

4.

5.

Commitment is a moment by moment practice. When we live the 100 percent committed life, we are truly living fully. Think about being committed to whatever you are doing in the present. When you are coaching warm-ups, commit to being fully present coaching warm-ups; when you are talking to an athlete, commit to being fully present with that athlete.

Living the 100 percent committed life means not multi-tasking. Multi-tasking is always a division of presence and can be felt by anyone you are in contact with.

Today, practice being 100 percent in the present with every task and interaction.

Mantra:
*I am 100 percent committed to what
I am doing at this moment.*

情熱

Day Six
DISCIPLINE

"Discipline is the bridge between goals
and accomplishment."
—Jim Rohn

Every great leader exhibits discipline. Discipline is doing what you should do, when you should do it, whether you like it or not. It is requiring yourself to do what you want your athletes to do.

This includes showing up on time and being prepared for the day, following through on the commitments you practiced yesterday, and most importantly, disciplining your mind and emotions.

Emotional control is one aspect of discipline that is essential for the ultimate leader. It is being able to notice when your thoughts and emotions are going into places of anger or frustration and doing whatever it takes to get to higher ground. It is noticing how you feel when you get stressed and slowing it down, using breathing and calming self-talk. It's doing EXACTLY what you would want your athletes to do if they feel fear, frustration, or competition nerves. It is impossible to have an atmosphere of respect, productivity, and positivity when the people you are leading are always afraid of what you are going to do next and if you are going to lose it. So many times emotional outbursts from coaches come from wanting it too much. The question is, do you really want it enough to create a healthy atmosphere for you and your athletes? Take a second, breathe, and get creative about whatever is frustrating you. You'll find the change in your athletes to be much more lasting when it's not based out of fear but in the desire to be better.

You must always model the appropriate behavior you want in the people around you, whether it be athletes, directors, or staff. Never expect your people to perform in ways you are not performing yourself.

Where are the places in your life that you lack discipline? Is it your temper, working out, self-care, creating workout plans for the day, or emotional control? Do you find yourself nagging about the same things over and over again in practice? Today, practice being disciplined and creative in one of those areas.

Make a commitment and write it below:
Today I...

Mantra:
I am disciplined in my thoughts,
words, and actions.

大胆不敵

Day Seven
ENTHUSIASM
"Nothing great was ever achieved without enthusiasm."
—Ralph Waldo Emerson

This is one of my favorite words. Here are a few definitions of our word of the day:

Inspiration as if by a divine or superhuman power; ecstasy; hence, a conceit of divine possession and revelation, or of being directly subject to some divine impulse.

A state of impassioned emotion; transport; elevation of fancy; exaltation of soul; as, the poetry of enthusiasm.

Enkindled and kindling fervor of soul; strong excitement of feeling on behalf of a cause or a subject; ardent and imaginative zeal or interest; as, he engaged in his profession with enthusiasm.

Lively manifestation of joy or zeal.

The word "enthusiasm" comes from the Greek words "en theos" = in God, or being inspired or possessed by the divine. So, who wouldn't want a "possessed" coach! As the ultimate leader, you want to possess the highest level of life energy and passion that you can muster up. But beware; you must always use your enthusiasm for good and not for evil!

This enthusiasm can be felt every day by those around you as your purpose and life's mission. Enthusiasm is contagious and definitely a good kind of contagious! How do you stay enthusiastic in a world that can be draining and stressful? Today, look at these keys to enthusiasm and spread the word to all around you.

1. Recognize the passion in whatever you are doing. If it's conditioning, be passionate about conditioning; if it's drills you've done 1000 times, be excited about them! If you are at practice, really enjoy your experience and see each moment as precious in its own crazy way!

2. Remember why you started coaching. Create two words that can become your purpose statement. It might be to "inspire excellence," or "raise self-confidence," or "create joy." Put these two words where you can see them this week and use them as a litmus test. Compare your thoughts, words and actions to your purpose and see if they pass the test!

3. Practice self-care. You can't be full of passion and energy when you are on empty.

4. Give your enthusiasm away. Be supportive of those around you. Be excited about their accomplishments, no matter how small. See how you can make everyone you come in contact with feel special. Notice how much power you feel when you empower others!

Mantra:
*I am enthusiastic and communicate
my energy to others.*

Day Eight
FEARLESS

"There is only one you for all time. Fearlessly be yourself."
—*Anthony Rapp*

Few people would argue that a Leadership Samurai leader would need to be fearless. The question is, how is that type of courage manifested day in and day out? What does it mean to be a fearless coach?

The bottom line is that the amount of fearlessness a coach has is proportional to the amount of respect they have from the people they lead. This is not the type of courage it takes to jump out of an airplane or behave recklessly; it is the warrior courage of living your values, overcoming adversity with grace, giving 100 percent, and being vulnerable.

Living with this type of fearlessness requires stepping beyond ego and insecurity. Not all leaders are brave enough to do that. It takes courage to face our fears and doubts, and to then act. It is natural to want to do what is easy, practiced, habitual and polished. It is natural to follow the path of least resistance.

Yet to lead with integrity, to learn quickly, to generate and share knowledge, and to make changes in our work life requires moving through the fear, uncertainty and discomfort of changing our thinking and behavior.

The following are five acts of fearlessness characteristics of the superior leader and coach:

1. The courage to take responsibility even when they are not directly responsible.

2. The courage to deal with conflict in a direct, honest, and kind manner.

3. The courage to be creative and take risks in order to break out of comfort zones and create change.

4. The courage to be open to feedback and respond without defensiveness.

5. The courage to act congruent with their values, no matter what the consequences.

Today, ask yourself two questions: What scares you? What are you afraid the people around you may see or say about you? Are you afraid to fail or not be good enough? (That's actually three questions!) Write the answers below or on another sheet of paper. Ask yourself each of these questions at least ten times and write the first response that comes to your mind. Here are some examples of responses:

I'm afraid to look stupid.
I'm afraid my business will fail.
I'm afraid I'm not good at what I do.
I'm afraid my athletes will not perform well.
I'm afraid people will see I don't really know what I'm doing.
I'm afraid people will think I don't know what I'm doing.
I'm afraid people will get angry with me and leave.

Mantra:
I trust life. I have nothing to fear.

Day Nine
GRATITUDE

"As we express our gratitude, we must never forget
that the highest appreciation is not to utter words,
but to live by them."
—*John F. Kennedy*

Gratitude is a practice that can melt away fear, worry, and
armor like no other, both in yourself and those you serve.
Gratitude is more than just saying, "Thank you." Gratitude is
a way of life, an energy that is pervasive throughout your
entire being.

Living in gratitude means looking at life through the eyes of
a child and seeing with wonder all the marvelous things in
this world. It is appreciating all that life has to offer—the joys
and the sorrows, the times you want to jump for joy, and the
times you want to collapse in pain. Gratitude is a celebration
of life itself.

When you coach in gratitude you can see the blessings in the
most frustrating times. You may find yourself smiling inside
as you have to work that athlete through the same correction
AGAIN. Whenever you feel stressed, find your way to freedom
through gratitude. Say to yourself, "I love this crazy sport"
and remember all it has given you. It's the good times and the
bad that make our work beautiful.

Look at your life. Marvel at how awesome it is. See the miracles
happening all around you. There is so much to be grateful for

every day: The people in your life, the friends who brought you joy, and the ones who taught you painful lessons. Today, take nothing for granted. Imagine what the world would be like without your car, the heat or air conditioning in your house, or the flowers that line your walkway. Take a moment to notice things you generally take for granted. Give silent thanks for all the things they bring to you.

When we live in gratitude, our joy spills over on others. We celebrate others' successes as we do our own. This is Gratitude with a capital "G." Not simply being thankful for circumstances that serve you and your ego, but "sympathetic gratitude" for all others.

Mantra:
I live today in gratitude.

Day Ten

HUMILITY

"You shouldn't gloat about anything you've done; you ought to keep going and find something better to do."
—*David Packard, CEO Hewlett-Packard*

The dictionary defines humility as modesty, lacking pretense, not believing that you are superior to others. Samurai leaders direct their ego away from themselves to the larger goal of leading those around them to greatness. These leaders are a complex, paradoxical mix of intense professional will and extreme personal humility. They will create amazing results, but shun public adulation and are never boastful. They are described as modest.

We often confuse humility with timidity. Humility is not hiding and having low self-esteem. Humility is all about maintaining our pride about who we are, about our achievements, about our worth – but without arrogance. It's about being content to let others discover the layers of our talents without having to boast about them. It's about giving the credit to your athletes or staff as well as yourself. It's a lack of arrogance, not a lack of aggressiveness in the pursuit of goals.

Humility is being open to learning from others, even those you consider less senior or experienced than you. It's about seeing value in everyone: The young coach and the old, the parent and athlete, the staff member who has been with you two months or ten years.

Great leaders treat everyone with respect regardless of position. When an idea is introduced, they are open-minded and curious instead of always protecting their point of view. They spend more time willing to learn from what others have to offer. They have moved away from pushing into allowing, from insecure to secure, from seeking approval to seeking enlightenment. They forget about being perfect and enjoy being in the moment.

Today, practice humility:

1. Let someone else take the credit or at least share the credit. Don't one-up with what you did or how you "made it happen."

2. Practice saying, "What a great idea!"

3. Listen without lecturing.

4. Seek input about situations that could be improved at your work and how you are doing.

Mantra:
I have nothing to prove.

Day Eleven
IMPACT

"As a coach, you must always be aware of the influence you have on your players. An incidental cutting remark, which you forgot about as soon as you said it, can stay with that young person and be a source of pain for a longer time than you may ever know."
—*John Wooden*

Imagine yourself like an energy imprint. With every thought, word, and action, you leave your signature on the people around you, especially your athletes. Some people are more susceptible to your imprint than others. People that are younger, have lower self-esteem, and see you in a power position are very influenced by your imprint. It's almost as if the athletes you work with are balls of Silly Putty and you are the comic strip they are stretched out upon. They take on your words and actions, and these can remain upon their minds and hearts for their entire lives.

You are making a huge impact on the people you come in contact with every day. The words you say stick, creating beliefs that your athletes will hold about themselves. What kind of impact do you want to make? What kind of life lessons are you teaching with your behavior? Here are some negative imprints to be wary of. Of course coaches don't do these things con-sciously, but these behaviors send messages that are engrained in their athletes' minds and bodies:

You are never good enough.
I only care about you when you do well.
If you make mistakes you will get punished or I will withdraw from you.

Your pain and injuries don't matter to me.
If you are not at the top you are not worth my time.
I don't believe you.
I am mean to you because I love you so much.
You're slow.
You're lazy.
You're not a hard worker.

It's essential that coaches take their level of impact seriously, because these messages can last a lifetime and affect their athletes long after they are done with sport. You have the amazing opportunity to teach positive messages that can frame the way the athlete sees the rest of their life. Things like:

All challenges make you stronger.
With hard work you can get better at anything.
Go all out and the rest will take care of itself.
I love you no matter how you perform.
Mistakes are learning opportunities.
It's okay to be sad, but then get up and take action.
No matter what, you are enough.

The words you use as a coach are extremely important. Words have power. Their impact is real and felt. Can you inspire your athletes without beating them down? Inspiring your athletes to change behaviors comes from a place of "I believe in you" or "I know you can be better, I've seen it." When you tear down your athletes, the underlying message is "you are not good enough. I don't know what to do with you." Today, strive to even deal with difficult issues with inspiration, not degradation.

Never forget how powerful you are in the lives of your athletes. As much as their parents, you are shaping their future and the belief systems they have about themselves.

Mantra:
I impact my athletes positively every day.

Day Twelve
INTENTION

"Leadership is the wise use of power. Power is the capacity
to translate intention into reality and sustain it."
—*Warren G. Bennis*

Every moment you make a choice. Every moment is filled with
intentions. And every moment these choices and intentions
create your life and contribute to the people you lead.

When your days drift by without setting intention for what
you want and who you want to be, your life becomes direc-
tionless, without much structure or purpose. Today, decide
and develop a laser-like focus on who you want to be and the
necessary actions to make it happen.

Sit quietly alone for a moment and answer these two questions:

Who do I want to be today as a coach?

Example: I am relaxed and confident. I have emotional control
no matter what happens around me. I am warm and ask others
personal questions that help them feel seen and important.
I take care of myself and only say yes to things I know I can
follow through with. I make a difference in people's lives by
inspiring belief in all those around me.

What do I want to accomplish today?

Be sure you set intention for your practice. Create a practice plan and walk into the gym with intention. When your athletes feel that you are prepared and organized, they can rise to your expectations.

Mantra:
I step into who I am as a leader with thought, word, and action.

歡喜

Day Thirteen
JOY

"Joy is a net of love by which you can catch souls."
—*Mother Teresa*

The Samurai leader communicates joy not only in what they do, but in life itself. Joy goes beyond happiness. Happiness and pleasure can be transitory, especially if based upon changing moods and outside circumstances.

Joy springs from deep within the soul when we are expressing our authentic self—our purpose. When we are on purpose in our work, our life is filled with joy. Accordingly, when we are filled with joy, our life is on purpose.

Don't hold yourself back from what makes you truly joyful, and find the joy in the ordinary of every practice. Stifling your joy is surely a slow death and a dark cloud to those around you.

Joy is contagious. As a coach, when you live your life with enthusiasm it radiates to all around you. How can you not feel joy on a day like today? Your bank account could be empty, your car in the shop, and your athletes are falling everywhere... and yet, you're alive! Be joyful about it. Decide that today is the day to express joy to all around you. You might as well, because tomorrow you may not be here.

Find the joy in the mundane moments. Take a mental snapshot of the beauty around you and know there will never be another moment just like this one. You will never be in this space, with these athletes, these coaches, doing this exact workout. You might as well enjoy it.

Dig deep. What are you doing with your life? What excites you? Where's the buzz? Life itself is what you've got going for yourself. So are you living in joy?

Many people, in fact perhaps most people, live at a survival level. Others live a mundane, boring life. What are you living? So many people are using up their precious moments of life striving for a bigger house, newer car, winning a state championship, and many additional outer expressions of the so-called necessities of life.

Joy is essential for you to feel alive in your coaching. Commit to being joyful in your Samurai life today.

Mantra:
I choose to live in joy.

Day Fourteen
KNOWLEDGEABLE
"It is possible to fly without motors, but not without knowledge and skill."
—*Wilbur Wright*

Knowledge is power. The ultimate leader has knowledge about the sport they love, the people they serve, and the procedures that make it all work together. The more information they have, the better they are at understanding their sport and those around them. Others look up to a knowledgeable leader, knowing they can learn and further their own career by following in their footsteps.

A great coach shares knowledge openly, empowering others to take their own level of performance to new heights. Utilize the resources available to you. If you don't know the answer to something, find out by asking questions. A leader must create access to information. Knowledge alone can't make a leader, but it can undo one. An incompetent coach has almost unlimited opportunities to be ineffective. Knowing what to do—coaching competence—is vital.

Being knowledgeable doesn't mean that a leader knows how to do everything, but rather that they know what to do and how to get it done. Even the most brilliant leader who tries to do it on their own is setting themselves up for failure. A good leader will know where their strengths and weaknesses lie and, thus, know what kind of expertise they will need to surround themselves with.

They utilize the many resources available to them: colleagues, the internet, conferences, articles, books, and websites. A good coach seeks out information to continually make themselves better. They know that there is always more to learn and are hungry for it.

Today, be sure you are well-informed about your sport. Do something to increase your knowledge and personal growth. A coach who is always growing in knowledge will be growing in respect.

Mantra:
I commit to growth every day.

Day Fifteen
LISTENING

"We have two ears and one mouth so that
we can listen twice as much as we speak."
—*Epictetus*

A good coach is a great listener. So many times people simply want to be heard. When they are heard they feel valued and important. This is true of athletes, parents, and fellow coaches.

Sometimes it is best to say nothing. Just listen. You see something going on with your athletes; just listen. You have a parent coming in for a meeting; just listen. A member of your staff needs to vent; just listen. Communication would be improved if sometimes we just shut our mouths and engage in what Buddhist monk Thich Nhat Hanh calls "compassionate listening."

"Compassionate listening brings about healing," he writes. "When someone listens to us this way, we feel some relief right away. We have to learn to do the same in order to heal the people we love and restore communication with them."

To listen compassionately is to listen deeply to another's words, to try to understand what meaning they are trying to express, without judgment or reservations, without mentally planning our advice or rebuttal while we are listening. It is not always easy to do, but compassionate listening will change your relationships in ways you cannot imagine.

So many times we don't really listen to what's going on with our athletes. We like to lecture, and we already have a preconceived idea of what they are going to say. Maybe we've already decided they are just going to whine, make excuses, or tell us how they can't do something. When you feel the most impatient is the time you should listen the hardest. Simply ask your athletes, "What's going on?" or "How can I help you today?"

Today, find three people who you can truly listen to. Practice listening without dismissing their point of view or planning what you are going to say next.

Mantra:
I listen to others with an open mind and heart.

Day Sixteen
MOTIVATION

"Motivation is a fire from within. If someone else tries to light that fire under you, chances are it will burn very briefly."
—Stephen R. Covey

Do you wake each morning excited to begin your day? Or do you face your work with dread? If you are just in it for the paycheck, you may find your motivation to coach fills you with anxiety instead of enthusiasm. If we want to feel motivated at leading others, we must feel as if our work is a reflection of our purpose. Remember your two words from Day Seven. When you know that every day is a chance to live that purpose, your motivation to coach is stronger.

When your work is on-purpose, you feel excited, fulfilled, and as if your life has meaning. Only then are we motivated to get up every day. One of the most important tools to create motivation in yourself and others is passion. Passion is a great motivator. It is what gives the ultimate meaning to your actions.

Being fiercely passionate about goals and targets helps give you and your athletes direction. However, passion has to be handled with precision and care. You don't want to use it to say and do things that are not productive or constructive in the gym. I have seen many passionate coaches be extremely destructive. Your athletes are motivated by many things. They are motivated to reach goals, work through challenges, and make others proud. How can everything you say be motivation and not destruction? One way is motivating through solutions. With every correction, be sure you are telling your athletes what you want them to be doing instead of focusing on what they aren't doing or the problem. When you continually harp on the problems and mistakes you are seeing, motivation goes down, both for you and your athletes! When you focus on what you WANT to see, your athletes have something positive to focus on. This keeps them motivated to try to achieve the goal of the turn or practice. When you motivate with optimism, enthusiasm, and positivity, your athletes feel that excitement as well and everyone feels more motivated, including you.

Today, be motivated and motivating. Remember why you coach and bring the passion to the gym. Motivate your athletes with solution-focused coaching. Make every correction be what you want to see instead of what you don't want to see. Nagging on mistakes or bad habits in the gym only brings everyone down.

Mantra:
I am motivated and motivating today.

精神圏創生

Day Seventeen

NOOGENESIS

"The great awareness comes slowly, piece by piece. The
path of spiritual growth is a path of lifelong learning. The
experience of spiritual power is basically a joyful one."
—*M. Scott Peck*

"What is it?" you ask. Noogenesis is the fourth of five stages
of man's evolution, described by French scientist and
philosopher, Pierre Teilhard de Chardin. It is defined as the
emergence of mind and self-reflection leading to the growth
of consciousness—the coming into being of the "noosphere."

Noosphere is defined as the sphere or stage of evolutionary
development characterized by (the emergence or dominance)
of consciousness, the mind, and interpersonal relationships.
We will look at Noogenesis as the part of the Samurai coach
and leader that is self-reflective, aware of his own thoughts,
and conscious of interpersonal interaction.

Can you be conscious of your thoughts and how they affect
others? Can you separate yourself from the field trips of your
mind and self-reflect on how they do or do not serve you?

The mind is most often the thing that gets you into the most
trouble. Only when you can reflect enough to separate yourself
from your thoughts can you truly be free and be a great leader.
A leader taken by the whims of the mind and ego is always
stuck in quicksand trying to get out. The quicksand deepens
and deepens as every effort to escape is met by an equal

intensity of pulling you under. The ultimate leader is able to watch his own mind from the bank of the chaos. Awareness and self-reflection are the ropes we throw to ourselves from the stable ground of freedom.

Today, watch your thinking. Notice which thoughts represent your highest vision of yourself and which do not. Delay action on any thought that does not represent who you want to be as a coach. Show courage and discipline not to fall into the quicksand.

Mantra:
I observe my thoughts without being swept away by them.

楽観主義

Day Eighteen
OPTIMISM

"Optimism is essential to achievement, and it is also
the foundation of courage and true progress."
—*Nicholas Murray Butler*

The servant leader is optimistic. The quality of optimism is
someone who is positive, most often seeing the glass as half
full instead of half empty. Optimistic people are more likable
and fun to be around than pessimists who are always the
"buzz kill" of the party.

Optimism is an emotional competence in a coach that can
help boost goal achievement, enhance morale in the gym,
and even overcome drama. In writing about optimism, you
face the danger of being seen as advocating a "Pollyanna" or
quixotic approach. The truth is, however, that optimism has
been proven to be a powerful tool that will pay dividends for
your personal life and give you a competitive advantage in
your sport.

There is a lot to be gained, indeed, in cultivating an optimistic
outlook. Take leadership, for example. Nowhere is optimism
more important than in leading athletes. Highly effective leaders
have a transforming effect on the athletes and staff around
them. They have the gift of being able to convince people
that they have the ability to achieve levels of performance
beyond those they thought possible. Isn't that what we want
our athletes to think and feel about themselves? They are
able to paint an optimistic and attainable view of the future

for their followers. They move others from being stuck in "the mistakes I've made in the past," and help them see "how things could be done better."

Relentless optimism is one of the key things we need from coaches to inspire us to achieve greatness. It's the idea that if we don't give up we can achieve our goals. And that someone as important to us as our coach believes it, too.

Today, instead of starting your day with the anxiety of all you need to get done, begin with a statement of positivity and optimism. Statements like, "I know my day will evolve exactly as it needs to," and "I'm excited to see what happens today," facilitate a mental state of flow rather than a state of force.

Psychologist Mihaly Csikszentmihalyi compares the state of flow to what sport psychologists call being "in the zone." Beginning your day with optimism begins it in this state of flow instead of stress, worry, and negativity. Use rituals of breathing, positive self-talk, enjoying your morning coffee, or reading something inspirational to put yourself in a mental state conducive to achieving your best results as a coach today.

Mantra:
I see everything that happens today with relentless optimism.

現行

Day Nineteen
PRESENT

"The most precious gift we can offer others is our presence.
When mindfulness embraces those we love, they will bloom
like flowers."
—*Thich Nhat Hanh*

Your mind can only focus on one thing at a time. As much as
you may think multi-tasking saves time, it is actually shaving
off precious minutes of your day, not to mention compromising
the quality of your task or interaction. There is nothing less
productive than thinking about many projects, tasks, and
conversations while focusing on none. The great coach is
present. They are 100 percent engaged to whatever they are
doing in the moment. That is living the fully present life.

The Sutra of Mindfulness reads, "When walking, the practitioner
must be conscious that he is walking. When sitting, the
practitioner must be conscious that he is sitting. When lying
down, the practitioner must be conscious that he is lying down."

So if we take the Sutra to heart, when e-mailing, we are
conscious of e-mailing. When working on next season's plan,
we are conscious of next year's plan. When talking to a staff
member, we are conscious of talking to that staff member.

When you are 100 percent present with what you are doing,
your creative genius shines through. It is when your ideas are
freshest and your listening skills unsurpassed.

Your crazy mind sets up a constant internal chatter, calculating and scheming, quarreling and debating, remembering wrongs against me and mine. The mind loves to run away from tasks into daydreams, to wander far without warning into past or future, only to return when it pleases.

Today, bring your mind back from these "field trips" by focusing on your breathing or using a key word or phrase. Saying something like "back to the present," or "now" can help reel your mind back into where it can be the most effective. Commit today to be fully present to whatever activity you and your athletes are engaged in during a specific moment.

Mantra:
I am 100 percent committed to this moment.

Day Twenty
QUALITY

"Quality means doing it right when no one is looking."
—*Henry Ford*

Great coaches know what qualities they value in themselves and others. They also recognize the importance of quality behaviors and habits. The best leaders exhibit both the qualities they value and personal ethics in their leadership style and actions.

Your leadership ethics and qualities should be visible, because you live them in your actions every single day. A lack of trust is a problem in many gyms when the coach doesn't live the qualities they preach.

If coaches never share their values with their athletes and staff, the mistrust is understandable. People don't know what they can expect. Every day or practice is unpredictable. Sometimes the coach is behaves one way, sometimes another. If coaches have identified and shared their values, and live these qualities daily, they will create trust. To say one sentiment and to do another will damage trust, possibly forever.

The following are examples of leadership qualities. You might use these as the starting point for clarifying the qualities you want to embody every day: *ambition, competency, individuality, equality, integrity, service, responsibility, accuracy, respect, dedication, diversity, improvement, enjoyment/fun, loyalty, credibility, honesty, innovativeness, teamwork, excellence, accountability, empowerment, quality, efficiency, dignity, collaboration, stewardship, empathy, accomplishment, courage, wisdom, independence, security, challenge, influence, learning, compassion, friendliness, discipline/order, generosity, persistency, optimism, dependability, flexibility.*

Quality also means the care you put into every thought, word, and action. Living a life of high quality means you have attention to every detail, being aware of the fact that quality (or lack thereof) becomes your brand.

Do people see you as a quality person? Do they consider your work to be detailed and attended to? The Samurai leader pays attention to these details, understanding that what is visible on the outside is a reflection of the person who created it.

Today, write your top five values that you want exemplified by your leadership.

1.

2.

3.

4.

5.

Mantra:
Quality on the outside reflects quality on the inside.

RESPONSIBLE

"Responsibility is the price of greatness."
—*Winston Churchill*

You are the creator of your life and everything in it. An amazing leader is one who takes responsibility for their part in all that occurs in life. They exemplify honesty, humility, and strength as they own whatever role they have in the situation.

What if you saw every opportunity as an opportunity to step up into greatness? What if you saw everything that occurred in your life as a "set-up" from the universe to test you and see if you could be the leader you were meant to be?

The ultimate assumption of responsibility in your life is accepting that the person, place, or thing that has triggered you is simply the result of a wound within you. If you feel upset by an event, try to see the message for you in that event. How can you learn? How can you grow? You have the power to create your life with your thoughts, actions, choices, perceptions, and beliefs.

Give up the blame game. As a coach, it's essential that you give up focusing on what a problem your athletes are. If they have fear, are moving slow, or not showing the kind of effort you like, how can you be creative and solve the problem? Can you teach a new drill, create a contest to change a habit, or reward the athletes that are working hard? Look at how you can take responsibility, get creative, and solve the problem.

When you take responsibility and see the gift in adversity, then you become extremely powerful.

You are responsible for every action you take. That is the meaning of karma—a simple law of cause and effect. For every action there is a reaction. Every action you take leads to a reaction from someone or something, which leads to your next action and so on and so on.

Today, acknowledge your part in all things. Catch yourself in any blame and look at what you have done to create a part of the situation and how you can fix it. You may be surprised at what you find.

Mantra:
I take responsibility for my life.

Day Twenty-Two
SERVICE

"How wonderful it is that nobody need wait a single moment before starting to improve the world."
—*Anne Frank*

You are more than the job you have. You are more than your role as a husband, wife, leader, coach, or teacher. Today, focus on the unique service you have been born to give to all those around you. The ultimate coach knows that sport is simply a vehicle they are utilizing in this moment to change lives. How can you be of service to the athletes you interact with every day? How can you instill belief, raise confidence, and empower the athletes and staff who look to you for inspiration? The Samurai leader is a servant first. You want to serve others. You see a lot of needs and want to make things better. The byproduct of this type of leadership is that the people you serve grow as people. They become healthier, wiser, happier, more creative, free, and more authentic to whom they really are. They also become better in their sport! Today, look at these characteristics of the Samurai leader, who could also be called a servant leader. Practice modeling this in the gym.

1. Be authentic: be yourself.

2. Be vulnerable: willing and able to put yourself out there, warts and all.

3. Be accepting: of the ideas, see the concerns of others as valid (even if not the best or brightest).

4. Be present: having your whole self there when needed, no distractions, listen.

5. Be useful: of service to those you are leading and serving.

Mantra:
How can I be of service today?

誠実

Day Twenty-Three
TRUTHFUL

"Most truths are so naked that people feel sorry
for them and cover them up, at least a little bit."
—*Edward Murrow*

How often do you lie? If we examine our words honestly, we will usually realize that we are perhaps not as honest as we think. We lie to avoid conflict. We lie to save our skin. We lie to make ourselves seem stronger and more important. How many times have you not told the "whole" truth in order to avoid confrontation or to save face? The ultimate leader tells the truth even when it's not easy.

Today, challenge yourself to find creative ways to be honest, even with difficult truths. Speaking honestly does not mean you should be harsh or cruel. We can learn to speak the truth in a way that the people around us can hear it, but we still must be loyal to the truth.

As a leader, it does not help the people surrounding you for you to be vague and dishonest about what you are seeing in them. They want your feedback. You have been put in a leadership position because your feedback has value. It robs all those around you when you hide or avoid the truth.

When you feel you must express a truth that may be either misinterpreted or hurtful, pause to first form a clear intention. Are you speaking because you wish to clearly communicate with another, or are you coming from a place of fear or the need to prove you're "right?" Remember, the more you can shove your own ego out of the way, the easier truth-telling will become. Focus on the other person's eyes and concentrate on communicating from the Samurai leader you are. Your purpose in telling the truth is always to serve.

With your athletes, find a way to speak the truth and still build self-esteem and confidence. It might be by expressing that they are not there YET but you know with hard work they can be. There are ways to tell the truth and not break your athletes' sense of self-worth.

In the space below, write the initials of two people to whom you avoid telling the truth. Challenge yourself to do it today. At the end of the day, think back over your words. Notice any time you caught yourself telling a lie. Ask yourself, "Why did I lie?" and "What am I afraid of?"

Mantra:
I am secure enough to tell the truth.

不動

Day Twenty-Four
UNSHAKEABLE

"Clear mind is like the full moon in the sky. Sometimes clouds
come and cover it, but the moon is always behind them.
Clouds go away, then the moon shines brightly. So don't
worry about clear mind: it is always there. When thinking
comes, behind it is clear mind. When thinking goes, there is
only clear mind. Thinking comes and goes, comes and goes.
You must not be attached to the coming or the going."
—*Zen Master Seung Sahn*

In my work with athletes, we talk about unshakeable mind.
Unshakeable mind means nothing gets to you. That you are
solid, stable, and rational amidst all adversity. The Samurai
leader shows calm in any storm. You are emotionally
disciplined and don't show a loss of control under pressure.

This type of discipline and emotional stability is essential if
you are to be a great coach. There is nothing worse than a
coach who is emotionally unpredictable. A lack of emotional
control can annihilate trust that has taken years to build. That
is just one reason to model unshakable mind. Your athletes
can tell when you are losing it in practice. It's essential to
teach your athletes to control emotions by modeling
emotional control yourself. This is true in your interactions
with athletes, other coaches, parents, and people outside
your gym.

We all follow a leader that shows fortitude under pressure.
We rely on these people to help us stay optimistic, calm,

and positive toward the future. In the turbulent world we live in today, it is even more important that our leaders display superior communication skills and emotional stability. In times of crises or when absorbing high doses of stress, you must at the very least appear to be under emotional control; otherwise other people will tend to lose confidence and faith in your abilities. This is especially important if other people are looking up to you, or you are seeking to influence others through your behaviors, decisions, or actions.

The key toward creating unshakable mind begins on the outside. You must first appear to others as though you are in full emotional control over yourself. This will give other people confidence in your ability to get the job done. The appearance of control is the critical first step toward regaining your balance. When others see that you are not shaken by your predicament, they will likewise maintain their poise and will better be able to assist you in this time of need.

Once you have established external emotional balance, you can now move onto the next step, which is centering yourself internally. To do this, you must learn to better understand yourself, as well as the events surrounding your situation. Any time you feel your unshakable mind is losing its grip, ask yourself the following questions:

Why am I feeling overwhelmed and stressed at this very moment?

How do I now choose to act proactively in response to these people, events or circumstances?

What strategies can I consistently use to ensure that I stay in this emotional, proactive state?

Mantra:
I am unshakable; nothing gets to me.

先見の明

Day Twenty-Five
VISION

"Your vision will become clear only when you can look into your own heart. Who looks outside, dreams; who looks inside, awakens."
—*Carl Jung*

Great coaches are visionaries. They see the possibility in all situations and don't get stuck in limitations. One of the greatest characteristics of good leadership is creativity to find solutions that have been overlooked. This is the power you have when you don't censor what you think, say, do, and believe.

A visionary doesn't censor. They express themselves and their ideas fully! They don't buy into negative belief systems that say, "This doesn't work," or "It can't be done." They forge ahead with a spirit of positivity and encouragement to others.

What ideas have you not acted upon? How does your self-talk and baggage from the past stop you from trusting your own creativity? How can you inspire your athletes with your vision?

What do you want? What do you want to create with your work, life, relationships, and sport? Today, create a mental picture of several aspects of your life evolving perfectly. Sit in a quiet space and visualize as clearly as possible whatever you want to create in your life: Coaching your best; Your athletes reaching their goals; Finding joy and balance in your life.

The power of vision is widely overlooked. Research has shown that what we put our mind on becomes manifest. The word manifest means "to become real." We teach athletes to visualize perfect performance, and perceive every element with excellence. Take this practice into your own coaching life.

Take the time to create what you want with visualization and the freedom in expressing your ideas.

Mantra:
I am aware of my creations.

Day Twenty-Six
WE

*"He who experiences the unity of life sees his own Self
in all beings, and all beings in his own Self, and looks
on everything with an impartial eye."*
—Buddha

We live in a very "me-focused" society. Most of us are running around worrying about me, mine, my, how do I look, how do they view me, what about me, me and more me! If you are to become the Samurai leader you must change "me-focus" to "we-focus."

Often we are so caught up in our own life dramas that we have no time to notice what is going on with others. We are all interconnected. There really is no me. Like drops of water in the ocean, we are all made up of the same stuff. We are beings of energy, and where "I" ends and "other" begins is more blurred than you might imagine!

Imagine walking into a room. Can you feel the energy of the other person? Does that energy affect you? Of course it does. Quantum physics has shown us that our combined energies are interacting at all times. Does the person at the front desk of the gym affect the back of the building where athletes are practicing? When you begin to think as a "we," you begin to see everyone's part in the divine creation. We all have our two-cents in the success and failure of any endeavor. There is no doubt that it takes a team to create any great organization.

In all your connections as a coach, an energy exchange takes place. You affect those you lead and they affect you. Are you building the people around you up or breaking them down? Notice not only the words you say but also your actions. When you walk away from another person, do they feel uplifted, or demeaned?

Today, in every interaction with your athletes or staff, notice how you feel afterward. You may feel a drain on your energy or a lift in spirit. Notice how others affect you but also ask yourself, "Am I an energy giver or an energy taker?" When you are aware, present, and interested in others, you most likely give them energy.

When you are judgmental, critical, and disapproving in your feedback, most likely you are an energy taker. A skillful coach can even give the most critical feedback in an energy-giving way when she focuses on honoring that person's gifts and finding a solution to the problem.

When you treat others the way you want to be treated, you are acknowledging the interconnectedness of us all. We are all just little baby humans for the most part, trying to make it work down here on the "loony balloon!" Today, notice how alike we all are.

Mantra:
We are the same.

案内者

Day Twenty-Seven
XENAGOGUE

"People are changed not by coercion or
intimidation but by example."
—*Anonymous*

If you have gotten this far, there is no doubt you were meant
to be a leader. Leaders are guides. Whenever we feel like a
stranger in a strange land, we look toward our leaders and
coaches for comfort, courage, and inspiration. A xenagogue
is defined as a guide; someone who conducts strangers,
showing them the way.

Think about the athletes you coach; you are their guide. How
do you guide them? What skills do you need to guide them
with care, compassion, inspiration and strength?

Guiding is also about mentoring. The people around you are
your present and your future. They can ease the worries of
today and are the resource of tomorrow.

The Zen story about teaching the people how to fish opposed
to simply feeding them fish is very applicable here. When
you mentor your staff and athletes, you provide them with
opportunities to learn, grow, experience challenges they
may face in the future, and have a relationship with you
that emotionally connects them to you. Mentoring sends
a message that you believe in your people and what they
can accomplish.

Being a xenagogue is rewarding for you, as well. It gives your work meaning and purpose, and at the same time sharpens your own skills. It's amazing how much mentoring someone can keep you on your toes. Many of us perform better when we know someone is modeling himself after us!

Today, be aware of ways you guide your athletes. They are looking to you as a role model.

Pretend as if everything you do is being observed and modeled by those you coach. Are you happy with the outcome?

Mantra:
I am a guide for my athletes and staff.

Day Twenty-Eight
YES!

"There is a life-affirming spark within you which constantly nudges you towards saying yes to life. Create your "yes" list; a list of all the things you want to say "yes" to, and be prepared to be amazed."
—*Lucy MacDonald*

Yes is one of the most important words in the English language. It comes from the Middle English word gese, meaning "so be it!" It's a word used to express great satisfaction, approval, or happiness. More importantly, it's this word that gives almost everyone a jolt of joy and confidence.

Are you a "no-person" or a "yes-person?" Do you always find reasons something won't work? Do you shoot down any new idea? Do you only talk about the mistakes? Yes has a powerful energy that resonates in the cells of every person on the planet.

Think of the difference between a person yelling "YES!" and a person yelling "NO!" It's amazing to actually feel how both of these words resonate in your body. It is said that a person who is told "no" too many times in their life becomes depressed, lethargic, and displays characteristics of what psychologists call "learned helplessness."

Learned helplessness is a psychological condition in which a person has learned to believe that they are helpless in a situation with no possible positive outcome. As a result, the person stays passive and even if change or escape is possible, they will not make an effort to succeed. With too many "no" messages, the people around you could potentially feel as if nothing they do is good enough.

The athletes around you want to hear how much you believe in them. The athletes around you want to feel your approval and support. Nothing communicates being on someone's side like a resounding "yes!" Even negative feedback can be heard and understood as a yes. When you give corrections by saying what you want your athletes to do, they feel your yes. It's the same when you express belief that even though things are bad now, you know they can get better. Even the worst practices can be turned around with the attitude of "yes we can!"

Yes also means taking risks in your life and as a coach. When you say yes to life, you are saying that you are ready for any experience life has to offer you. Saying yes cultivates fearlessness.

It's important that your yes comes from the heart, however. Saying yes, when what you want to say is no, is poison to your body. Yes to you might mean no to others.

Today, cue in to what you really want, behind your fear and your excuses, and say YES to who you are and what you want out of your day. Coach from a place of yes. Even if it's a bad day, find a way to express it with excitement and optimism.

Mantra:
I say YES to life.

生けるもの

Day Twenty-Nine: Bonus Day
ZOETIC

"We're so engaged in doing things to achieve purposes
of outer value that we forget the inner value; the rapture
that is associated with being alive, is what it is all about."
—*Joseph Campbell*

Definition of zoetic: living, vital, alive. Synonyms: breathing,
live, living, moving, viable, vital. Antonyms: dead, lifeless.

There is no more important word to end our four-week
practice. Are you zoetic? Do you feel really alive? Hopefully,
this practice has helped you wake up to whom you are as a
coach and what you want to give as a leader. My hope is that
it has ignited a sense of purpose and passion as you focused
each day on how you could make a difference to those
you serve.

Today, don't forget your aliveness. You are viable. You are
vital. You are zoetic.

What does it mean to be truly alive and move through
your life with energy and vitality? You dance in the rain.
Laugh at your mistakes. Stand in awe as the universe
presents you with the same challenges again and again.
And with everything that happens, big or small, happy
or sad, greet it with a resounding "bring it on!"

If you are still living in the body, you are a bringer of life.
Today, commit to bring life to the lifeless. There are so many

people suffering, feeling dead inside, victims of lives they have created and now hate. They're feeling as if their goals are out of reach. Being the wonderful zoetic coach that you are, it is your opportunity to breathe life into their stuckness by simply being kind and positive. It doesn't matter if they respond on the surface, because somewhere your aliveness is felt by them. Even if it is on a cellular level, you have brought some sun to their ice-age.

Today, commit to bring vitality to all you come in contact with. It really is the only thing to do.

Mantra:
*I bring aliveness to all those who come
in contact with me.*

THE BEGINNING

Go back to Day One.
You are the Samurai...aren't you?

With joy,
Ali